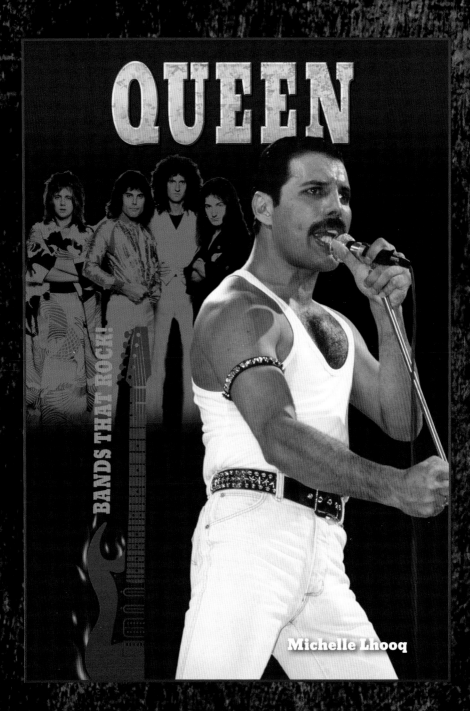

QUEEN

BANDS THAT ROCK!

Michelle Lhooq

Enslow Publishing
101 W. 23rd Street
Suite 240
New York, NY 10011
USA

enslow.com

Published in 2019 by Enslow Publishing, LLC.
101 W. 23rd Street, Suite 240, New York, NY 10011

Library of Congress Cataloging-in-Publication Data

Names: Lhooq, Michelle, author.
Title: Queen / Michelle Lhooq.
Description: New York : Enslow Publishing, 2019. | Series: Bands that rock! | Audience: Grades 7-12. |
Includes bibliographical references and index.
Identifiers: LCCN 2018012262| ISBN 9781978503519 (library bound) | ISBN 9781978505261 (pbk.)
Subjects: LCSH: Queen (Musical group)—Juvenile literature. | Rock musicians—England—Biography—Juvenile literature.
Classification: LCC ML3930.Q44 L56 2019 | DDC 782.42166092/2—dc23
LC record available at https://lccn.loc.gov/2018012262

Printed in China

To Our Readers: We have done our best to make sure all website addresses in this book were active and appropriate when we went to press. However, the author and the publisher have no control over and assume no liability for the material available on those websites or on any websites they may link to. Any comments or suggestions can be sent by email to customerservice@enslow.com.

CONTENTS

Queen performs at the Montreux Rock Festival in Switzerland on May 12, 1984. Lead singer Freddie Mercury was well known for his flamboyant, high-energy stage presence.

Introduction

Queen's "Bohemian Rhapsody" is one of the greatest songs of all time. When it was released in 1975 on October 31—yes, on Halloween—it was an immediate, smashing success. Shooting up to the top spot on the UK singles chart, the number one song stayed there for a whopping nine weeks and sold more than a million copies by the end of that year.

Over the years, the song's popularity didn't fizzle out—in fact, it only got stronger. It remains the third-highest-selling single of all time in the UK, and you still hear the song blasting out of karaoke rooms and car windows all over the world. The musical roller coaster remains just as exhilarating no matter how many times you ride it.

By all musical standards, "Bohemian Rhapsody" is really, really weird, which is why it's such a historical quirk that the song managed to find so much commercial and radio success. At six minutes long, it's twice as long as the average pop song, and it doesn't have a chorus or a catchy hook. In fact, the song structure is wildly unpredictable; one of the most distinctive things about "Bohemian Rhapsody" is that is sounds like four or five different songs in a row.

It opens with the band crooning the song's surreal refrain—"Is this the real life?"—and then moves into a piano-driven power ballad, with the band's charismatic lead singer, Freddie Mercury, getting increasingly emotional and dramatic. A wailing electric guitar solo provides a brief interlude before segueing into a playful and dramatic opera. *And then* it dives into a head-thrashing hard rock section, finally circling back to the power ballad where it all began, as Mercury repeatedly croons, "Nothing really matters to me." It ends with the crash of a gong.

"Bohemian Rhapsody" was written over a seven-year period by Mercury and recorded in just three weeks—with one week devoted to the opera section. In the studio, all four members of the band would often sing into one mike, with their voices layering on top of each other to create a uniquely rich, echo-like effect. Nobody really knew what the finished song would sound like except Mercury.

Roy Thomas Baker, a producer on the album, remembers when he heard the song for the first time. "I was standing at the back of the control room, and you just knew that you were listening for the first time to a big page in history," he said.[1] He was right.

While there are many theories about what the song is about, nobody really knows what Mercury was thinking when he wrote this epic masterpiece. The lyrics contain a grab bag of references spanning all kinds of different artistic traditions, cultural figures, and languages, including the Spanish flamenco dance called the fandango, the famous astronomer Galileo, the first word in the Qu'ran, and the Italian expression of surprise "mamma mia!"

"I think people should just listen to it, think about it, and then make up their own minds as to what it says to them," Mercury once said, and the rest of the band is keeping their lips sealed.[2]

In many ways, "Bohemian Rhapsody" captures what's so exceptional about Queen. It's artistically profound and wildly experimental, yet completely accessible and radio-friendly. It's the kind of fun, crowd-pleasing anthem that you can wail along to with all your friends at your birthday party or school dance. But it's also the kind of contemplative, richly detailed song that you can sit down with and listen to carefully, alone in the dark in your room. Most of all, it's completely and utterly original. We'll probably never have another band quite like Queen, but their story lives on forever.

Before They Were Queen

Before Queen got together as a band, the members spent their early years in various places around the world, living in vastly different circumstances. In order to understand how the group came to be, it is critical to first learn about their childhoods—a formative time that shaped their characters but did not define them.

Freddie Mercury (Lead Vocals, Piano)

Freddie Mercury came into this world on September 5, 1946, as Farrokh Bulsara and was born on the small spice island of Zanzibar, off the east coast of Africa. His family were Parsis (descendants of Persians), and his father was employed by the British government, working as a cashier at the British Colonial Office.

In 1954, when he turned eight, Farrokh's parents shipped him off to St. Peter's English boarding school in Panchgani, about 50 miles (80 kilometers) outside Bombay, India. It was there that he picked up the nickname "Freddie" from his friends. At home, Freddie loved singing along to records on his family's record player. Noticing his natural talent for

Konde

Njao Island

Kish Kash

Fundo Island

Wete

Kojani Island

Mzambarauni

Tanga

Uvinje Island

Pemba

Misali Island

Wesha

Chake Chake

Limani

Makoongwe Island

Mkoani

Kengeia

Pemba Channel

Matumbini Island

Kiweni Island

Pangani

TANZANIA

Tumbatu
Island

reefs

Mkokotoni

Ngava

ZANZIBAR

Zanzibar Channel

Mangapwani

Unguja

Bububu

Koani

reefs

Zanzibar

Chwaka

Jozani

Paje

Uzi

Kwale Island

Uzi Island

Kikutani

Pungume Island

Mkunguni

INDIAN OCEAN

Unguja and Pemba are the two
main islands of the Zanzibar
Archipelago, which is part of
Tanzania.

Bagamoyo

Dar es Salaam

0   10   20   30 km

"You have no idea how mega I am going to be!"

music, his school's headmaster encouraged his parents to let him take on extracurricular music classes. They agreed, and Freddie started taking piano lessons and joined the school choir.

But music wasn't the only thing that Freddie excelled at. He was a school champion at table tennis at age ten, acted in the lead role for various school plays, and spent most of his free time sketching and painting. His many talents were recognized with a "Junior All-Rounder" trophy from his school when he was eleven, and he won a prize for "Academic Prowess" the next year.

When Freddie was twelve, he formed his school's rock band, the Hectics, with five of his friends—Derrick Branche, Bruce Murray, Farang Irani, and Victory Rana. The group would play at school parties, with Freddie jangling away on the piano. From a young age, Freddie was confident over his star potential."I am going to be mega! You have no idea how mega I am going to be!" he told his friends at the boarding school.[1]

After Freddie graduated from high school, he returned to Zanzibar for two years. But the country was in the throes of extreme political unrest, with the Zanzibar Revolution occurring in 1964. That year, the Bulsara family moved to Feltham in England to escape the violence and social turmoil.

Seventeen-year-old Freddie wanted to go to art school, but first he had to pass his qualifying exams. So he enrolled at a nearby polytechnic school, and during his vacations, he did all kinds of odd jobs—from working in the catering department of Heathrow Airport to lifting and stacking crates at a warehouse in the Feltham trading estate. All the while,

Freddie Mercury poses at a photo shoot in London, England, in 1973.

Zanzibar Revolution

In December 1963, Zanzibar won independence from England. One month later, on January 12, 1964, local African revolutionaries, led by John Okello of the Afro-Shirazi Party, overthrew the sultan of Zanzibar and the government. These African revolutionaries were fueled by frustration over their lack of political representation, believing that the sultan's government was run by Arab and Indian businessmen who were unfairly put in power by the English colonialists. Following the revolution, the country erupted in ethnic violence, resulting in a death toll estimated to be between several hundred to twenty thousand. Facing persecution, many civilians fled to other countries, including the Bulsaras, who were of Parsi (Persian) descent.

he was dreaming of a different life—one in which he knew he would play a starring role.

Brian May (Lead Guitar, Vocals)

Brian Harold May was born in Hampton, England, on July 19, 1947, as the sheltered only child to Scottish-English parents. Tall, lanky, and well-spoken, May became known as one of the most influential, innovative, and technically gifted guitarists in the history of rock music. May was also a versatile

Brian May, pictured here in 1974, fell in love with the electric guitar early in his life.

songwriter, penning many of Queen's biggest hits—including some of their harder and more aggressive songs like "We Will Rock You," as well as emotional ballads like "Save Me."

Brian went to Hampton Grammar School, where he excelled in physics and mathematics. His love for music was inspired by his father, who played the piano and banjolele, a four-stringed instrument that resembles a banjo. But Brian desperately wanted to play the guitar, so when he was seven, his parents scraped together enough money to buy him an acoustic one. Before long, Brian had turned it into an electric guitar by plugging it into a homemade amplifier.

"At 16, I was desperate for a proper electric guitar, but there was no way we could afford it, so Dad and I started making one," May said. His father worked at the Ministry of Aviation as an electronics engineer, developing the landing system for the Concorde jet, and was a skilled technician. "Dad could make anything," May noted. "He converted our spare bedroom into a workshop where he made all our household appliances including our TV."[2]

Over eighteen months, the two of them fashioned together a guitar using hand tools and any materials they could get their hands on. They made the neck of the instrument with parts from an old fireplace, carved the fret markers—the circles along the neck between the metal strips—out of mother-of-pearl buttons, and used a bicycle saddlebag holder for the arm, topping it off with the tip of one of his mother's knitting needles.

"It was a special time and we never really argued," May recalled of this time with his dad. "We had no idea how big a part the [guitar] would play in my life—I thought I'd just have fun with it at home."[3] This guitar—which May called "The Red Special" after the color of the wood it was made from, or "the old lady" when he was feeling especially affectionate— stayed with him for the rest of his life. May went on to use it for every Queen album and live show, often playing it with a sixpence coin.

In 1964, when he was seventeen, Brian formed a band with his friends named after George Orwell's novel *1984*. They rehearsed regularly at a school in Twickenham and put on their debut performance at the nearby St. Mary's Church hall later that year, playing a blend of pop, R&B, and soul covers. "In retrospect, 1984 was lightweight, a bit fluffy," admitted Tim Staffell, the band's singer. "It was impossible not to be naively ambitious—that was part and parcel of it—and the primary motivation to do it was what we saw in the media as the end results of success. But I guess we were realistic about it—we were at school, after all. Also there was a good deal of pressure in the 60s from our parents, and the conservative generation, to conform."[4]

When Brian moved to London in 1965 to attend Imperial College, studying physics and astronomy, he brought the band with him, playing regular shows at school, including an opening gig for Jimi Hendrix. As 1984 started to take off, a reporter from local newspaper the *Chronicle* calling them "one of the most forward-looking groups today."[5] In 1967, the group joined a battle-of-the-bands competition at a club in Croydon, just south of London, and took home the top prize. But increasing musical differences and the pressures of schoolwork caused the members to drift apart, and in 1968, May left the band, followed by Staffell a little later.

Later that year, May, who was turning into an exceptional guitarist, decided to start a new band with Staffell, who played bass and sang. They called themselves Smile, playing the sort of improvisational style that British rock bands such as Cream were popularizing at that time. They also began sniffing around for other musicians to join them—not yet knowing that they were paving the path for history.

Cream was an influential 1960s rock group made up of guitarist/singer Eric Clapton, drummer Ginger Baker, and bassist/singer Jack Bruce. Their music spanned psychedelic rock and the blues and helped to popularize the wah-wah pedal—a type of electric guitar pedal that alters the sound's tone and frequency in order to create a "wah-wah" sound. Cream is often called the world's first "supergroup" because of the fame of each of its members, and they influenced bands like Led Zeppelin, Black Sabbath, the Allman Brothers Band, and Lynyrd Skynyrd.

The members of Queen were highly influenced by Cream, pictured here in 1968. From left to right are Eric Clapton, Ginger Baker, and Jack Bruce.

Roger Taylor (Drums, Vocals)

Roger Meddowes Taylor was born in Norfolk, England, on July 26, 1949. Handsome with a rowdy streak, he had a flashy sense of showmanship—often coating the skins of his drums with a white powder during shows so that once he started playing, he'd be surrounded in a white, hazy cloud.

Born to a middle-class family, he loved music from a young age, forming his first band, the Bubblingover Boys, with some friends when he was seven years old, playing the ukulele.

In 1957, when he was eight, Roger and his mom, dad, and younger sister Claire moved to Cornwall, a summer resort area in southwest England. He attended the Truro Cathedral School, where he sang in the local choir. He also switched from playing the ukelele to the guitar, forming a band called The Cross.

In 1961, his dad bought him a drum, and Roger realized he was a natural after teaching himself to play by listening to drummers from bands like the Who and the Jimi Hendrix Experience.

"I took to it and started adding to it and found I could get along well. I found myself getting better quite quickly, so that sort of spurred me on," he said. "It was at that point that I became a drummer rather than a guitarist—which I'd always wanted to be before. I think everybody wants to be a guitarist, but I'm a better drummer than a guitarist anyway."[6]

At age fifteen, he started playing rock music as the drummer for a Cornwall band, the Reaction, which was made up of boys from his school. When their singer left, Roger even took a turn on lead vocals for a stint.

When he turned nineteen, Roger really wanted to move to London, so he took a course in dentistry at London Hospital Medical College. He quickly got bored and decided to switch schools, studying biology at East London Polytechnic. But at heart, Roger was a drummer—one with blistering intensity

Roger Taylor started out playing the guitar, but after he discovered he had a knack for the drums, he could not envision himself doing anything else.

who'd go down in history as one of the best ever. Ever since he was a kid, he'd dreamed of playing in a great rock and roll band. He just needed to figure out how.

John Deacon (Bass Guitar)

John Richard Deacon, known to his friends as "Deaks" or "Deaky," was born on August 19, 1951, into a middle-class family in Leicester, England. In sharp contrast to his more flamboyant bandmates, John was extremely quiet and shy and could often be counted on as the calmest presence in Queen.

 "I listened to a lot of soul music when I was in school."

His father worked at the Norwich Union insurance company, and the family moved to the town of Oadby when John was nine. A top student, John coasted through his classes in school, easily finding time to pursue his hobbies of music and electronics. In 1963, when he was twelve, he replaced his old toy guitar with his first real instrument: a six-string acoustic guitar. The next year, the Beatles shot to the top of the charts, and John Lennon became one of his musical idols. John quickly became an outstanding rhythm guitar player, and instead of using a guitar pick, he preferred plucking and strumming the strings with his fingers.

John was also really interested in electronics and built many of his own devices as a kid. He even built a modified tape deck that he'd use to record songs straight off the radio. "I listened to a lot of soul music when I was in school," Deacon recalled. "I've always been interested in that sort of music."[7]

He originally joined his first band, the Opposition, as a roadie and electrician, helping them set up and break down

Bass guitarist John Deacon poses for a photo in Mercury's apartment in early 1974. Deacon is known as "the quiet one" of the group.

their gear at gigs. He then joined as a guitar player. But the band's bass player's skills were soon found to be lacking, and John frequently had to fill in by playing the low bass notes on the bottom strings of his guitar. Eventually, the band convinced him to switch instruments and be their full-time bassist. So in 1965, John bought an EKO bass at a music shop in Leicester and took on the role. In the spring of 1966, he made his public debut, taking the stage for the first time.

Three years later, John left the group to study acoustics and vibration technology at Chelsea College in London. Little did he know that a chance meeting at a party would change the rest of his life.

Early Days

In 1966, when Freddie Bulsara turned twenty, he finally got what he'd worked so hard to attain: an acceptance letter to study graphic illustration from an art school in London called Ealing College of Art. At this point, Freddie was more than ready to spread his wings and move out of his parents' house. "I was quite rebellious, and my parents hated it," Freddie said. "I grew out of living at home at an early age. I just wanted the best. I wanted to be my own boss."[1]

Freddie moved into an apartment in Kensington in West London that was rented by his friend, Chris Smith. London was in the middle of the Swinging Sixties—a hedonistic era of creative revolution as the city emerged from the gloom of World War II to become an epicenter of style and culture. "It Girl" models such as Twiggy were strutting around in miniskirts as the faces of "mod" fashion. Bands like the Who, the Kinks, and the Rolling Stones were popularizing a distinctively raw and tough version of rock and roll as part of a cultural phenomenon

 **"I wanted to be my own boss."**

known as the British Invasion. It was an incredibly exciting time to be a young, creative person in London as all kinds of artists flocked to the city, and Freddie arrived there just in time to be at the center of it.

Coming Together

Like Freddie Bulsara, Brian May and Roger Taylor moved to London in the late 1960s for school. May was studying physics and mathematics at Imperial College London, where he was an excellent student, graduating in 1968 with honors.

Taylor originally came to the city to study dentistry at the London Hospital Medical College, but he quickly got bored

The British Invasion

Before 1964, only two British singles had ever topped *Billboard*'s Hot z100 chart. Everything changed with the arrival of the Beatles' number one song "I Want to Hold Your Hand."[2] The band played their first US show that year, kicking off a cultural phenomenon known as the British Invasion, where British rock and pop acts were enthusiastically embraced by American audiences in the mid- to late 1960s. The Who, the Kinks, and the Rolling Stones were London bands that represented a particularly tough, snarling, and rebellious approach to rock and roll.

and switched to biology at a different school. In 1968, Taylor saw a note posted on an Imperial College bulletin board for a band named Smile that was looking for a drummer, and he decided to audition.

"I remember being flabbergasted when Roger set his [drum] kit up at Imperial College," May said. "Just the sound of him tuning his drums was better than I'd heard from anyone before."[3] They accepted him into the band on the spot.

At the same time, Tim Staffell and Freddie Bulsara were becoming fast friends after meeting at Ealing College. Tagging along with Staffell, Bulsara started hanging out at Smile's band rehearsals and was quickly inspired to start experimenting with music for the first time since he had been a kid in India.

"The first time I heard Freddie sing I was amazed,"

remembers Chris, one of the friends whom Freddie started jamming with. "He had a huge voice. Although his piano style was very affected, very Mozart, he had a great touch. From a

The Who perform at the BBC TV Centre in London in 1966. From left to right are John Entwistle, Keith Moon, Roger Daltrey, and Pete Townshend.

Freddie (*standing fourth from right*) takes a photo with the many members of Ibex in Bolton, Lancashire, on August 23, 1969. It was his first professional job as a musician, and he had not yet adopted the surname Mercury.

piano player's point of view, his approach was unique."[4]

After Freddie Bulsara graduated from art school, he moved into Taylor's apartment. To make some money, they opened a stall together at Kensington Market, with Freddie selling his own artwork, along with new and secondhand clothes.

In the summer of 1969, Freddie was introduced to a band from Liverpool called Ibex, who shared his love for acts such as Cream, Jimi Hendrix, and Led Zeppelin. They clicked right away, and ten days later, Freddie hit the road with the band for a show in Bolton, Lancashire, having already picked up the band's set and contributed a few of his own songs. It was Freddie's first real gig, but he was already showing a preternatural talent for showmanship, oozing charisma out of every pore. With his flowing long hair, painted black fingernails, and cat-like prowl, he carried an exotic glamour with a whiff of danger. It was impossible take your eyes off him.

Roman God Mercury

In Roman mythology, Mercury was the son of Jupiter, king of all the gods. With his winged sandals, he could fly faster than all the gods and served as their trusted messenger. Mercury was known for being playful and a clever trickster. The word "mercurial" is also used to describe someone who is extremely unpredictable. With the two sharing many characteristics, this Roman god was the perfect inspiration for Freddie Mercury's alter ego.

The Roman god Mercury was the messenger of the gods. Hermes is the name given to his Greek counterpart.

"He knew how to front a show," said Ken Testi, Ibex's manager. "It was his way of expressing that side of his personality. Everything he did on stage later in Queen, he was doing with Ibex at his first gig."[5]

Freddie Bulsara renamed the band Wreckage, and they continued to play together for a few more months before fizzling out. So he went searching for a new musical act and became the lead singer of a band called Sour Milk Sea after answering an ad in a popular music magazine called *Melody Maker*. But that band also disbanded by the end of the year. Freddie then set his sights on Smile. He wanted badly to be their lead singer. Sometimes, at Smile's live shows, he would even yell out, "If I was your singer, I'd show you how it was done!"[6]

Regardless of his eccentricities, Freddie was completely serious about the way he approached music. He was convinced that putting on an entertaining show during live performances was extremely important—in fact, it was just as crucial to a band's success as its music.

"It's great how you're building up atmospheres and bringing them down," Freddie told Brian May. "But you're not dressing right, you're not addressing the audience properly."[7] To Freddie, every live show was an opportunity to connect with the crowd.

When Tim Staffell left Smile in 1970, Freddie seized the opportunity to join the band. He was already living in an apartment with May and Taylor, Smile's remaining members, by this time, so it only made sense for the three of them to regroup as a new band.

Brian May and Roger Taylor met John Deacon in early 1971 at a disco, when they were introduced by a mutual friend. They'd just lost their bassist and asked Deacon to try out for the position. A few days later, Deacon met the band in a lecture room at Imperial College. Even though he was

The band's logo is on display on the drum set as Roger Taylor performs at Wembley Stadium in 1992.

 **"Unless he knew someone well he could be shy."**

extremely shy and barely spoke during the audition, he played the bass perfectly, and they knew he was the missing link.

"In the early days I used to be very quiet because I always felt I was the new boy. But I think I fitted in because of that," said Deacon. "[Smile] tried several other bass players before me, but their personalities seemed to clash. I was all right because I wasn't going to upstage Brian or Freddie."[8] Deacon was hired on the spot, and the band was finally complete.

Taking Charge

Immediately, Freddie Bulsara tried to persuade everyone to dress in the flamboyant style that was popular then. He also wanted to change the name of the band. May and Taylor suggested names such as the Rich Kids and the Grand Dance, but Freddie was set on Queen. He thought it was a strong name that sounded both regal and universal. He also knew the word was open to all kinds of interpretations—including its use as a slang word in gay culture for drag queens.

Freddie Bulsara also started calling himself Freddie Mercury, a reference to the Roman messenger of the gods. The alias was key to helping him invent a new persona—the outlandish, larger-than-life character he wanted to be. Of course, he was still his old self to his friends and family. In fact, Mercury's friend David Wigg noted, "In contrast to his stage presence, unless he knew someone well he could be shy. But to the public, and especially on stage, he was going to be a god."[9]

Finally, Freddie Mercury used his graphic illustration skills to design the band's logo. Wanting to create a regal aura around the band to match its name, Mercury drew inspiration from the British monarchy's coat of arms in order to convey a sense of elegance, patriotism, and authority. He placed a crown inside the letter Q, with a majestic phoenix spreading its wings above. He also incorporated the astrological signs of each band members—two lions symbolized Leo (John Deacon and Roger Taylor), a crab for Cancer (Brian May), and two fairies for Virgo (Freddie Mercury). The Roman-style font was designed by Richard Gray, the band's longtime photographer and designer. The logo became one of the most iconic and widely recognized symbols in the history of rock.

Queen

studio to record new music, using the same high-end facilities as the Beatles and Elton John.

"They turned out to be every bit as good—and demanding—as we'd anticipated," Sheffield said. The process of recording their debut album took over a year, as the band had to figure out which of their tracks would be the best representation of their musical identity for their big debut. The band also insisted that every song had to be recorded their way until they deemed it perfect. "Things had to be one hundred percent right, otherwise they wouldn't be happy," Sheffield said.[2]

 "Things had to be one hundred percent right, otherwise they wouldn't be happy."

According to Sheffield, Queen would painstakingly obsess over every last detail, spending days and nights working on their vocal harmonies and other aspects of their songs. They would often argue over the littlest things, shouting and throwing things at each other. But in the end, they'd always manage to move on. "They'd always sort it out, however," Sheffield said. "It wasn't personal, it was about the work."[3]

The Debut

In 1973, the band finished their album and signed to two record labels that Trident had negotiated contracts with: EMI Records in the United Kingdom and Elektra Records in the United States. After rejecting potential titles like *Pix, Info,* and *Deary Me* (a favorite saying of Mercury's), the band decided to simply call their first album *Queen.* It was released in July 1973, with a simple yet striking cover of Mercury raising a

microphone above his head with both arms, standing under two stark purple spotlights.

Spanning genres such as hard rock, progressive rock, and heavy metal, songs such as "The Night Comes Down," "My Fairy Queen," and "Jesus," touched on subjects that the band would come back to over their career, such as coming-of-age, religion, and mythical folklore.

The album received decent reviews by local media. "Queen is England's latest candidate for superstardom, and don't be surprised if these guys do make it in a big way," wrote the *Winnipeg Free Press*.[4] However, the album was largely ignored by commercial radio and the mainstream media, reaching a disappointing number 32 and 83 respectively on the UK and US charts. Journalists seemed to think that, even though they had a fresh, energetic sound, Queen were mostly copying acts such as Jimi Hendrix and Black Sabbath.

Failing to conquer the charts motivated the band to return to the studio for their second album with more determination and focus. They decided to experiment with a wider range of sounds and inject their songs with sharper, ear-catching melodies. They emerged with their second album, *Queen II,* in 1974. The record showed that Queen was developing their signature sound: catchy pop hooks over heavy, thickly layered song arrangements and playful, quirky melodies. This time, the record reached number five on the UK charts, and its lead single, "Seven Seas of Rhye" became their first hit. However, critical reception in the press was still lukewarm; *Rolling Stone*, the most influential music magazine of the era, gave it only two and a half stars out of five.

Despite the lack of support from the media, Queen's popularity was growing thanks to the strength of their captivating live shows. In September 1973, they played their first live recorded gig in London, and the next month, they flew to Belgium, France, Holland, Germany, and Luxembourg

The Beginning

for TV appearances and concerts. In November, they opened for a band called Mott the Hoople and ended up impressing everyone so much with their dramatic live set that they were offered an opening slot on Mott the Hoople's next tour—this time, in America.

A Health Crisis

In 1974, Queen embarked on their first US tour with Mott the Hoople, where their growing following of adoring fans began shouting "God save the Queen!" at their concerts—a chant that followed the band throughout their lifespan. With their growing popularity, EMI decided to re-release *Queen*, and this time, it reached number 24 on the UK charts.

A month into the tour and after forty-one shows, May suddenly collapsed from pain. His health had been deteriorating since the end of 1973, when he had developed a high fever and contracted gangrene in his arm, which swelled up to the size of a football. Doctors weren't sure if they'd have to amputate it, but thankfully May had recovered enough to go on tour. Now it seemed that he

Queen rock the stage in 1974. That same year, they wowed American audiences on their first tour in the United States.

The Beginning

"We were devastated. The tour had been cut short . . . but also [we were] very worried about Brian."

was in trouble again. Doctors diagnosed him with hepatitis, a condition that he suffered from for the rest of his life.

It turned out that he'd been injected with an infected needle when the band got vaccination shots before going on tour. This unforeseen medical disaster forced Queen to cancel the rest of their shows so that May could return to London to recover. "Poor Brian turned bright yellow, and I was amazed we managed to shepherd him through the immigration queue

Hepatitis is a serious liver infection usually caused by the hepatitis B virus (HBV), although it is also linked to heavy alcohol use, certain medications, and other infectious diseases that infect the autoimmune system. In some cases, the virus does not show any physical symptoms, but in other cases, it can cause yellow discoloration of the skin and whites of the eyes, poor appetite, vomiting, tiredness, abdominal pain, or diarrhea. Hepatitis can be temporary, lasting less than six months, or long-term, and chronic hepatitis can increase risks of both liver failure and liver cancer.

at JFK in New York," said Taylor. "The poor fellow could hardly stand, and we got him on the plane, got him home, and got him to hospital. He was very ill."[5]

"We were devastated," Taylor continued. "The tour had been cut short, you know, so there were mixed feelings about that, but also [we were] very worried about Brian on the other hand."[6]

Ending their first major tour early was a major blow to the momentum Queen had been building, putting their future in peril. But May admitted that "in some ways it was a relief to get hep, even though I felt so bad physically."[7] Their first big tour had been grueling both mentally and physically, and everyone was feeling pretty run down. Now that they were back in England, the band could hole up in their studio to write and record their third album, which would become their first smash success.

an apartment in London with his girlfriend, Mary Austin, and most of the outside world assumed he was straight. But one night during the tour, Mercury's friend John Anthony, who was accompanying the band, was woken up by a phone call from Mercury summoning him to his hotel room. He found Mercury dressed in a nightcap and pajamas, hanging out with two girls. Mercury told Anthony to get rid of them. Once the girls had left, Mercury told Anthony that he was gay and wanted Anthony to break the news to Mary Austin. Anthony refused and retreated back to his room. But when the band returned to England, Mercury found another apartment for Mary Austin, whom he remained close friends with, and soon began a relationship with David Minns, his first serious male partner.

Going Global

Meanwhile, Queen's popularity was taking off internationally. In November, they went on their first European tour, starting in Sweden and going through Belgium, Germany, Holland, and finally, Spain. Queen was becoming particularly hot in Japan. Even though they hadn't played a single show there, their albums were flying off shelves. The country's leading music magazine, *Music Life*, had even named them as one of the best bands in the world. In 1975, they made their first trip to Japan, where three thousand fans showed up at the airport chanting the band's name.

But the more successful Queen became, the more they started to fight with their management over money issues. Trident had been advancing them equipment and salaries for the previous four years, and the band now owed the company

 **Three thousand fans showed up at the airport chanting the band's name.**

"Bohemian Rhapsody": The First Music Video in History

In November 1975, Queen decided to film a short video to accompany "Bohemian Rhapsody"—and unwittingly made what many historians now consider the first true music video ever. "We never had the idea that a song would only be represented by a video, it was just one way of promoting it," said May.[3]

But while other bands such as the Beatles had made promotional films for their songs in the past, "Bohemian Rhapsody" was the first time a movie-like, stylishly filmed video played a huge part in boosting a global hit's commercial success. With not much of a storyline or prior rehearsals, the video was filmed with a shoestring budget in four hours by director Bruce Gowers and aired for the first time on the popular TV show *Top of the Pops*. Despite its slapdash nature, the video still became extremely influential, helping to popularize the medium for generations of musicians to come.[4]

close to $280,406 ($2.45 million today). One day, Mercury demanded a grand piano. When Sheffield said no, Mercury became extremely upset, banging his fist on the table. "I have to get a grand piano," he insisted.[5]

When Sheffield explained that money from the band's tour and album sales hadn't completely hit the bank yet, Mercury protested: "But we're stars. We're selling millions of records. And I'm still living in the same flat I've been in for the past three years."

Sheffield informed him that the money would come in December, so he had to wait. Mercury stamped his feet and yelled. His reply would later become part of the

group's lore: "No, I am not prepared to wait any longer. I want it all. I want it now."[6]

In September 1975, the band split with Trident, success-fully negotiating themselves out of their debt. They had to

The members of Queen enjoy a pleasant and peaceful day in Tokyo, Japan, sitting in a hotel garden in 1975. They found great success even in countries where English was not people's first language.

The Wayne's World "Bohemian Rhapsody" Scene

Although you could still hear it on classic rock stations on the radio, by the early 1990s, "Bohemian Rhapsody" had largely faded from the public's memory. But in 1992, Mike Myers, the star of *Wayne's World*—a film based on a *Saturday Night Live* sketch of the same name—used the song in a particularly memorable opening scene and propelled it back into the popular consciousness. In the movie's opening scene, Wayne pops the song into the cassette tape player of his friend Garth's car, and the crew gleefully lip-syncs every word while cruising down the street. This simple yet memorable scene became instantly iconic, and the song started playing regularly on MTV, reintroducing it to a new generation of kids and propelling it to the number two position of *Billboard*'s Hot 100 in 1992.[7]

Dana Carvey (*far left*) and Mike Meyers (*far right*) reprise their roles as Wayne and Garth, in 1993's *Wayne's World 2*. The first movie put "Bohemian Rhapsody" back on the music charts.

Race to the Top

On September 18, 1976—the exact six-year anniversary of the death of Mercury's idol Jimi Hendrix—nearly two hundred thousand people, a record number, flocked to Queen's biggest show yet, an open-air concert at London's Hyde Park. As a thank you from the band to their loyal fans, the show was completely free.

Excitement was crackling in the air as the performance began dramatically, smoke bombs and elaborate lighting setting the scene with Queen's theatrical flair. Mercury, wearing a white leotard with a glittering crotch piece, ascended from below the stage in a billowing cloud of smoke. He greeted the roaring crowd with a shout: "Darlings!"

For the next eighty minutes, the band launched into an intense set that proved Mercury was a bonafide star who could stand shoulder to shoulder with the era's reigning musical stars such as David Bowie and Mick Jagger. "When I go on stage," Mercury said, "whether I'm rich or starving, I want to give my all. I want to go on there and die for the show!"[1]

Hurrying back to the studio, the band finished their next album *A Day at the Races*, which was the first record they produced

Roger Taylor and Freddie Mercury perform at the free concert they put on for their fans in Hyde Park 1976.

entirely by themselves. Released in December 1976, the album shared many similarities with Queen's previous release, *A Night at the Opera*. Both records featured the Queen crest as the cover art, and their titles were both references to movies by the American family comedy act the Marx Brothers. In fact, in March 1977, the most famous member of the Marx Brothers, Groucho Marx, even invited Queen to his Los Angeles home when they were in town for a show. The band thanked him in person for inspiring them by presenting him with a gold disc and performed an a cappella version song from *A Night at the Opera* called "39" at his request.

The album's biggest hit, "Somebody to Love," was written by Mercury with Aretha Franklin in mind. "It was a gospel way of singing, I was inspired by the gospel approach she had on her earlier albums," Mercury explained. In order to create that sound, Mercury, May, and Taylor spent a week in the studio, recording and layering their voices on top of each other to create an effect that sounded like a 160-voice gospel choir. It was a painstaking process, but the band had no regrets. "We are perfectionists about things and we think it's worth spending that time," said Mercury.[2]

The Punk Backlash

A Day at the Races was a huge commercial success, selling over five million copies worldwide and topping the album charts in the United Kingdom, Japan, and the Netherlands. But some critics in the media criticized the band for playing it too safe commercially, by delivering the same dramatic and elaborate style of rock as their last album, *A Night at the Opera*, without taking many artistic risks.

 **"If there's a challenge we embark on it and that's what keeps us going."**

The musical climate in the United Kingdom in 1976 and 1977 was undergoing a major shift. In response to the country's economic troubles and dwindling opportunities for the youth, a loud, aggressive style of punk music led by bands such as the Sex Pistols was emerging that stood in stark contrast to Queen's glamorous, larger-than-life version of rock. "The whole punk thing was a tough phase for us and I thought that was going to be it," Mercury said. "But if there's a challenge we embark on it and that's what keeps us going."[3]

The AIDS Crisis

Despite these big cultural shifts in the air, Queen was still wildly popular, and as part of their *Night of the Opera* tour in 1977, the band performed a sold-out show at Madison Square Garden in New York—a sign that they had truly broken through in America. Touring in the United States also allowed Mercury to escape the gaze of the British press, and he was determined to explore his sexuality as a gay man—an identity he had been hiding for a long time. He started going to gay bars in whatever city he was in, regularly picking up one-night-stands.

Mercury's carefree attitude toward sex was not uncommon in the 1960s and 1970s, especially among bohemian and artistic crowds. Most people at that time, including Mercury, didn't know about HIV and AIDS. That would soon change when the deadly virus became a national epidemic that forever changed society—and Mercury's life.

The rest of the band had been too preoccupied with their own lives offstage to pay much attention to Mercury's nighttime activities. May had gotten married and was spending most of his time with his wife, while Deacon's own wife and son had also accompanied him on tour. "The subject of Freddie's sexuality never came up because it wasn't even mentioned," May said.[4] It was only when the band members

Queen and the Sex Pistols

On December 1, 1976, Queen had to pull out of a scheduled TV appearance on London's *Today* show at the last minute because Mercury had to go to an emergency dentist appointment. They were replaced by the Sex Pistols, a hot new punk band that was also signed to Queen's record label, EMI. The Sex Pistols were extremely disruptive, responding to interview questions with expletives and causing a huge scene. This TV appearance launched them to national notoriety, which is why some people say that Queen gave the Sex Pistols their first big break—even if it was accidental.

started noticing men following Mercury back to his hotel room during the US tour that they realized he was no longer only having relations with women. But it wasn't an issue.

Queen released their sixth album, *News of the World*, in 1977, which contained many songs suited for massive arena performances, including two hits that would become anthems at sports events around the world, "We Will Rock

"The subject of Freddie's sexuality never came up because it wasn't even mentioned."

The Sex Pistols' lead singer Johnny Rotten performs at Dunstable's Queensway Hall, October 21, 1976. The punk scene was raw, raucous, and rebellious, quite the opposite of Queen's glittering outfits and soaring vocals.

Race to the Top

It is believed that HIV originated in the Democratic Republic of Congo around 1920, when the virus was transmitted from chimpanzees to humans. Before the 1980s, we do not know exactly how many people were infected with HIV. Some cases of AIDS were documented before 1970, but the epidemic started in the mid- to late 1970s. By 1980, HIV spread to North America, South America, Europe, Africa, and Australia, infecting between one hundred thousand and three hundred thousand people. In 1982, the Centers for Disease Control and Prevention (CDC) published a report about five young, previously healthy, gay men in Los Angeles with unusual infections and immune systems that were not working. It was the first official report of cases of AIDS, a term coined by the CDC in September 1982 that stands for "acquired immunodeficiency syndrome."

Activists march at a Gay Pride parade in New York City in June 1983. In the early 1980s, AIDS was not yet very well understood, and most people saw it as a "gay" disease.

You," and "We Are the Champions." Their next record, *Jazz*, didn't actually contain much jazz music at all. Instead, the 1978 release stuck to hard rock sounds and power ballads, with Mercury's over-the-top vocals and May's majestic guitar playing.

In order to promote "Fat Bottomed Girls" and "Bicycle Race," the lead singles on *Jazz*, Queen rented out Wimbledon Stadium for a day and hired sixty-five female models to stage a nude bicycle race around the venue. Video footage from the stunt was later used in a promotional video for "Bicycle Race," but it was a poster with a photograph of the race that came with the album as a fold-out that stirred up the most controversy. Due to public outcry, the poster was banned in the United States, and subsequently, fans who bought the album had to mail in a special order form if they wanted the fold-out sent to them.

On Halloween that year, the band threw a party in New Orleans to celebrate the release of *Jazz*. More than four hundred celebrities, friends, and groupies attended the wild event, which featured strippers, mud wrestlers, drag queens, and a jazz band. Both the nude bicycle race and the crazy New Orleans party fueled Queen's growing reputation as one of rock and roll's wildest and most extravagant stars.

Disco Downfall

Throughout the 1970s, Queen was moving away from the progressive and glam rock influences that had defined their earlier albums and started adopting a more mainstream pop sound. In the summer of 1979, wanting a change in scenery, the band relocated to Munich, Germany, to record their next album at Musicland Studios, where acclaimed bands such as Led Zeppelin, the Rolling Stones, T. Rex, and Deep Purple had also recorded their music.

The studio was founded by the famous disco producer Giorgio Moroder, and it was there that Queen met the renowned German producer/engineer Reinhold Mack, whom everyone just called Mack. Mack was known for pulling off ingenious little tricks while in the studio; for example, he would often stick mics on the inside of the drums so that they'd sound extra crisp and big, filling up the room without overwhelming the rest of the instruments.

One of the first tracks that Queen recorded at Musicland was called "Crazy Little Thing Called Love," a catchy 50s-style rockabilly track that sounded like something Elvis Presley would have sung. Unlike Queen's other songs, "Crazy Little Thing Called Love" was stripped down and simple—it did not feature Mercury's over-the-top vocals or the band's usual multi-layered instrumentation.

Mercury wrote the track while taking a bath at the Hilton hotel in Munich. "We arranged the song at band rehearsals the following day with me trying to play the rhythm guitar," said Mercury. "The finished version sounded like the bathroom version. It's not typical of my work, but that's because nothing is typical of my work."[1] Although the band was still working on their album, their label decided to release the song as a single. It went to number one in America and took second place on the British charts.

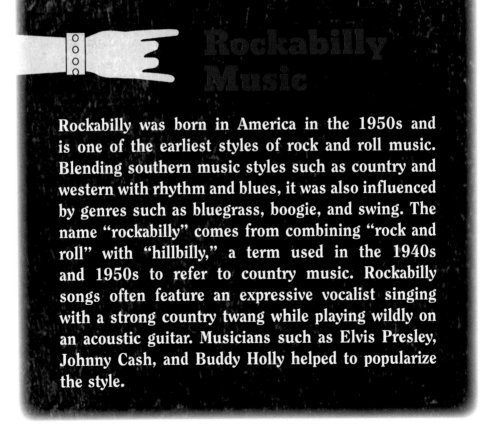

Rockabilly Music

Rockabilly was born in America in the 1950s and is one of the earliest styles of rock and roll music. Blending southern music styles such as country and western with rhythm and blues, it was also influenced by genres such as bluegrass, boogie, and swing. The name "rockabilly" comes from combining "rock and roll" with "hillbilly," a term used in the 1940s and 1950s to refer to country music. Rockabilly songs often feature an expressive vocalist singing with a strong country twang while playing wildly on an acoustic guitar. Musicians such as Elvis Presley, Johnny Cash, and Buddy Holly helped to popularize the style.

"We all tried to leave the band more than once."

The band continued to work on their album in 1980, continuously arguing and butting heads in the process while driving each other nuts. "We went through a bad period in Munich. We struggled bitterly with each other," May said. "We all tried to leave the band more than once. But then we'd come back to the idea that the band was greater than any of us. It was more enduring than most of our marriages."[2]

Munich Nightlife

Occasionally, the band would take breaks from the studio and each other to immerse themselves in Munich's thriving nightlife scene. Unlike their experiences on tour—where they would only stay in each city for a few days—the band was able to become regulars at local hangouts in Munich, going back to the same clubs every night. "We were very much influenced by what was going on in the clubs. A lot of that was assimilated and put into the record," said May.[3]

The band loved hanging out at one club in particular called the Sugar Shack—a venue they even later referenced with a song called "Dragon Attack." "It was a rock disco [club] with an amazing sound system," May said. "The fact that some of our records didn't sound very good in there made us change our whole perspective on our mixes and our music."[4]

On June 30, 1980, Queen unleashed its eighth record, *The Game*—the most accessible and pop-oriented album it ever made. In addition to "Crazy Little Thing Called Love," the release also included another chart-topping single called "Another One Bites the Dust," a disco/funk tune that featured one of the most memorable bass melodies in the history of music.

Freddie Mercury performs in the
Netherlands in November 1980.

The title of the song was inspired by a common phrase used by cowboys, "to bite the dust," which means to suffer defeat or death. Cowboys also served as the inspiration for the lighthearted lyrics written by Deacon. The song was heavily influenced by funk music—a genre invented in the 1960s and popularized by African American musicians such as James Brown, Parliament Funkadelic, and Chaka Khan.

One of the biggest early fans of "Another Bites the Dust" was Michael Jackson, who heard the song one night while he was hanging out backstage at a Queen show in Los Angeles. Jackson recognized its potential to be a major hit right away. "I remember Michael and some of his brothers in the dressing room going on and on about 'Another One Bites the Dust,'" said Taylor. "They kept saying we must release it as a single."[5]

The song became a crossover hit in America, entering both the R&B and pop charts (where it stayed in the number one position for three years) and establishing Queen as one of the the most popular bands in the world.

Perhaps inspired by their experiences in Munich's disco scene, the band also started using a synthesizer for the first time on *The Game*, breaking a "no synths" rule that they'd established for their previous seven albums. Taylor bought a state-of-the-art synth and showed it to Mercury. After that, Queen began to use electronic sounds made with synths more and more on their records throughout the 1980s.

The David Bowie Years

Queen began to work on their next album, *Hot Space*, in 1981 in Munich. That summer, they were joined by David Bowie, who dropped by the studio for an unplanned drug- and alcohol-fueled jam session that ended up lasting for twenty-four hours and produced another major hit. "'Under Pressure" was based on a particularly memorable guitar riff that Deacon had come up with and Bowie had helped to tweak. Each band

A synthesizer (often called a "synth") is an electronic musical instrument first used in pop music in the 1960s. They are extremely versatile and can be used to imitate traditional instruments like the piano, organ, or flute and natural sounds like ocean waves and wind, or they can be used to create their own unique and futuristic electronic sounds. Synths were popularized in the late-70s thanks to disco music, and they became linked to electronic music pioneers such as Kraftwerk, David Bowie, and Yellow Magic Orchestra. The instrument continues to be used heavily in genres such as pop, hip-hop, and dance music today.

This is a classic analog synthesizer. Synthesizers have been an important part of pop music since the 1960s.

member then went into the vocal booth and sang how they thought the melody should go, improvising as they went along. Together, they put together all the different sections to make it a cohesive song, working on the lyrics as a team. "I still cannot believe that we had the whole thing written and recorded in one evening flat," said Bowie. "Quite a feat for what is actually a fairly complicated song."[6]

 **"I still cannot believe that we had the whole thing written and recorded in one evening flat."**

As soon as Queen's record label heard that the band had recorded an impromptu song with Bowie, they rushed to put it on the airwaves. "Under Pressure" became Queen's second number one single in the United Kingdom, following on the heels of "Bohemian Rhapsody" six years prior. The song also became a Top 10 hit in eleven other countries, but it only reached number 29 in the United States.

While Queen remained popular in other parts of the world, their increasingly electronic-influenced disco and funk sound turned many people in America against them. At the time, the United States was experiencing a major backlash against disco, which was seen as overly fluffy and decadent. Many of Queen's fans wanted them to return to their earlier hard rock sound. "I think *Hot Space* was a mistake, if only timing wise," May admitted. "We got heavily into funk and it was quite similar to what Michael Jackson did on *Thriller*. But the timing was wrong. Disco was a dirty word."[7]

Mercury was particularly sensitive to the poor reaction that the album had gotten. "*Hot Space* was one of the biggest risks we've taken, but people can't relate to something that's

"Under Pressure" was an unplanned yet epic collaboration between Queen and David Bowie, pictured here in 1982.

Disco Downfall

outside the norm," he said. "I think it was way ahead of its time."[8]

Queen found themselves in a strange situation. They were playing sold-out concerts in massive stadiums all over the world, including in South America, Japan, and Australia, but their demand in America was plummeting. For the next nine years, Queen would not be able to clinch a Top 10 hit on the American charts. "It was a very sad thing," said May. "I remember Freddie saying 'I'll probably have to . . . die before America wants us."[9] Tragically, Mercury's words would one day prove true.

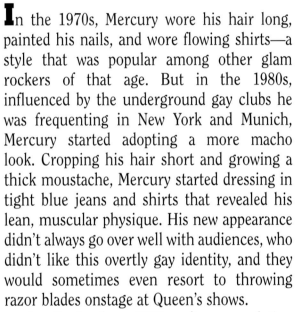

"The Greatest Day of Our Lives"

In the 1970s, Mercury wore his hair long, painted his nails, and wore flowing shirts—a style that was popular among other glam rockers of that age. But in the 1980s, influenced by the underground gay clubs he was frequenting in New York and Munich, Mercury started adopting a more macho look. Cropping his hair short and growing a thick moustache, Mercury started dressing in tight blue jeans and shirts that revealed his lean, muscular physique. His new appearance didn't always go over well with audiences, who didn't like this overtly gay identity, and they would sometimes even resort to throwing razor blades onstage at Queen's shows.

In September 1982, after completing their North America tour, Queen flew to New York City to record a performance for *Saturday Night Live* at Rockefeller Center—what became their final performance in the United States as a group. Singing and playing the acoustic guitar while performing "Under Pressure" and "Crazy Little Thing Called Love," Mercury appeared pale and out of breath. He told others that he had a bad

Freddie Mercury traded in his white jumpsuit for a red silk bomber jacket in 1984. His style evolved into a more traditonally masculine look.

flu, upset stomach, and severe headaches. He'd also seen a doctor the previous month for a white-colored sore that had mysteriously appeared on his tongue. Mercury assumed that he was just under the weather from his party-heavy lifestyle. Little did he know that he was exhibiting all the common early signs of HIV.

Unaware of his life-threatening condition, Mercury continued to live his extravagant lifestyle. In 1984, he rented a lavish five-bedroom house in Los Angeles. The band was spending a few months in California working on their next album, marking the first time they'd recorded a record in America. To celebrate his thirty-seventh birthday—and give everyone a break from the studio—Mercury threw himself a party at his rented house, filling it to the brim with huge red and pink lilies and serving all his favorite food to a hundred guests.

By 1984, the world had woken up to the fact that HIV was spreading dramatically—7,699 cases of AIDS were reported in the United States that year, with 3,665 fatalities. Hospitals were both underequipped and underinformed on to deal with AIDS, and because of the stigma attached to homosexuality, patients often had to deal with the worst kinds of discrimination. Some researchers even refused to work on the disease because of its association with the gay male community.

"It was just an avalanche," said Cleve Jones, founder of an AIDS memorial project in Atlanta. "It was like one week, we'd never heard of it, and then the next week, everybody started to die. People began to vanish."[1]

Later that year, the band returned to Munich to finish their album. Mercury threw himself into the party scene with even more recklessness than before—perhaps because he had begun to suspect (or accept) that he'd contracted HIV. By this time, Queen had grown unhappy with their previous record label Elektra and had negotiated their way out of the contract,

"The Greatest Day of Our Lives"

signing with Capital Records in the United States instead. Part of their agreement with Capital included a solo record deal for Mercury, which he would work on privately, in between studio time with the band and his late-night partying.

The Works

At the end of 1984, Queen released their eleventh album, which they decided to call *The Works* because it had just about every kind of song that you'd expect from the band—including love ballads, rock anthems, and German-influenced electro-pop. Its lead single, "Radio Ga Ga," was written by Taylor, who was inspired by his infant son. The album was a success in the United Kingdom, reaching number two on the album charts, but it performed even worse than *Hot Space* in the United States, much to the band's disappointment.

In addition to the music, American audiences rejected a music video Queen had made for "I Want to Break Free," another lead song on the album. In the video, the four band members all dressed in drag, wearing women's clothing, wigs, and accessories, playing characters that referenced a popular British soap opera called *Coronation Street*. While European fans understood the video and its references, Americans were far less accepting. MTV even banned the video entirely. "In America, [the video] wasn't accepted at all well because they still regarded us as the heavy rockers there—the macho thing," said Mercury. "They reacted with, 'What are my idols doing dressing up in frocks?'"[2] Still, Mercury believed it was one of their best music videos ever made.

In 1985, Mercury released his solo album, *Mr. Bad Guy*. The record ranged from emotional ballads about sadness and pain to more light-hearted, tongue-in-cheek tunes. It performed well on the UK charts but received lukewarm reviews. Mercury, however, was proud of his work and thought it represented both the sensitive and fun-loving sides of

Freddie Mercury performs at the Rock in Rio festival in Brazil in 1985, wearing his costume from Queen's controversial "I Want to Break Free" music video.

"The Greatest Day of Our Lives"

his personality. "I put my heart and soul into [*Mr. Bad Guy*]... I think it's a very natural album," he said. "I think the songs reflect the state of my life; a diverse selection of moods."[3]

Queen's lackluster chart performances and struggle to win over US audiences—combined with the fact that both Mercury and May had released their own solo efforts—started to spark rumors that the band was on the verge of breaking up. The members themselves seemed unsure of their future. But one of the biggest and most ambitious rock concerts in history would soon seal the fate of the band.

Live Aid

Bob Geldof was an Irish singer-songwriter who led a rock band called the Boomtown Rats in the late 1970s and early 1980s. In 1984, struck by news reports about a famine in Africa, he'd cowritten a song called "Do They Know It's Christmas" to raise money for the crisis. The song became the United Kingdom's biggest-selling single of the time, raising millions of dollars. Motivated by his song's success, Geldof planned a benefit concert on a scale that world had never seen before.

Billed as "the Global Jukebox," Geldof's Live Aid fundraiser would take place in two stadium arenas at the same time—Wembley Stadium in London and JFK Stadium in Philadelphia—with performances also happening in Japan, Australia, Holland, Yugoslavia, Russia, and Germany. The sixteen-hour, one-time-only show of live music would be broadcast to 1.9 billion people across 150 countries, making it one of the largest-scale television broadcasts of all time. Of course, the success of the stunt hinged on the quality of the performances, and Geldof enlisted some of the biggest rock stars in the world to join the lineup.[4]

When Geldof approached Queen, they thought it was an impossible feat to pull off, but they agreed—partly because they wanted to support the good cause, but also because so

Criticism of Live Aid

In its July 1986 issue, *SPIN* magazine published an investigative story called "Live Aid: The Terrible Truth," which revealed that the money Live Aid had raised was being funneled to Ethiopian dictator Mengistu Haile Mariam, who was using it to buy weapons and slaughter hundreds of thousands of people as part of an ongoing civil war. In his autobiography, BBC's Andy Kershaw also criticized the concert's predominantly white, male lineup of rock stars, writing, "Musically, Live Aid was to be entirely predictable and boring. . . . [I]t became clear that this was another parade of the same old rock aristocracy in a concert for Africa, organised by someone who... didn't see fit to [include] on the Live Aid bill a single African performer."[5]

many iconic acts were participating that it was impossible for them to miss out. In what might be the most epic concert lineup in history, Live Aid's final bill included Bob Dylan, David Bowie, U2, Madonna, Led Zeppelin, the Rolling Stones, and many more.

They squabbled over the set, whether to play the hits or try something new. In the end they did the hits. Known for spectacle with expensive backdrops and lighting rigs, they had to purely rely on their skills with the stadium's sparse background. "After 13 years do you still get excited about this kind of live performance?" asked a reporter at a press conference before the show. "We still like to play... and fool around," replied Mercury with  a smirk. Next, the reporter asked if they thought, with so many superstars in the same place, there would be a battle of egos. "It's going to be chaotic. We're not all well-behaved kids," Mercury grinned. "But that's going to be the nice part,

Queen's 1985 performance at Live Aid went down as one of music history's most memorable moments.

actually. We're all going to try and outdo each other." He paused for a split second before playing it cool. "Well... we're just going to go out there and play."[6]

And play they did. From the second Mercury sat down at his gleaming white piano to sing, "Mama, just killed a man," the opening lines of "Bohemian Rhapsody," Queen was full steam ahead. Their taut, energy-packed set on July 13, 1985, packed six of their greatest hits—"Bohemian Rhapsody," "Radio Ga Ga," "Hammer to Fall," "Crazy Little Thing Called Love," "We Will Rock You," and "We Are the Champions"— into twenty minutes, with one song often blending into the next like a seamless medley. The TV cameras couldn't get enough of Mercury, who strutted back and forth, soaking up the attention and commanding the audience to sing and clap along. By the end of the set, one thing was clear: Queen had completely conquered the hearts of everyone watching.

"Queen were absolutely the best band on [that] day," said Geldof. "It was the perfect stage for Freddie."[7] Even Elton John confronted the band as they came offstage, shouting that they had stolen the show.[8]

The Foo Fighters' Dave Grohl agreed. "Queen smoked 'em. They walked away being the greatest band you'd ever seen in your life, and it was unbelievable," he recalled. "And that's what made the band so great; that's why they should be recognised as one of the greatest rock bands of all time— because they could connect with an audience."[9]

"That was entirely down to Freddie. The rest of us played okay, but Freddie was out there and took it to another level," May marveled many years later. "It was the greatest day of our lives."[10]

Made in Heaven

CHAPTER 8

Their success at Live Aid was the second wind that Queen desperately needed. Their previous albums experienced a surge in popularity, entering the charts again. By September, they were back in Munich working on a new single called "One Vision"—a song celebrating universal love that was inspired by their experience at Live Aid, as well as by Martin Luther King Jr. "I got a sort of newfound force," said Mercury. "Suddenly, there was more left of Queen."[1]

Mercury also celebrated his thirty-ninth birthday in his signature extravagant style, flying out many of his three hundred guests from London to Munich. The birthday ball was held at his favorite local club, Henderson's, which he'd rented out and completely redecorated.

A Changed Man

But Mercury was changing as the reality of his HIV-positive status sunk in. No longer able to deny the results of medical test after medical test, he was going out to gay nightclubs less and less frequently and spending more time at his mansion in London, Garden Lodge. Toward the end of 1985, he abruptly abandoned his life, friends, and lovers in Munich without warning and moved back to London, where he surrounded himself with his closest friends and his longtime boyfriend, Jim Hutton. "I've stopped going out, stopped the nights of wild partying. I've almost become a nun," Mercury said. "Once, I was extremely promiscuous, it was excess in every direction, but now I'm totally different."[2]

Mercury threw himself into recording Queen's next album, *A Kind of Magic,* which they released in March 1986. It went straight to the top of the UK album charts, becoming their first number one album to do so since 1980. The band went on a UK and European tour, even returning to the site of their Live Aid appearance, Wembley Stadium, to play two sold-out shows.

During the tour, Mercury struggled with throat problems, including nodules on his vocal chords that made it painful for him to sing. His entourage also started to notice his lack of desire to party. "Fred was much more settled," recalled a former keyboardist of Queen's. "He didn't have the taste for going out clubbing and staying up all night, the way he used to."[3] Instead, the keyboardist and Mercury would often retreat back to the hotel after shows to play board games until sunrise.

On August 9, 1986, Queen finished their tour with a grand finale in London, playing to a crowd of 120,000. They played a twenty-six-song set that spanned their entire career of hits. At the end, Mercury, dressed in a regal robe, held up a crown to the audience before taking a bow. It was a fitting salute to what turned out to be Queen's final show together, although no one in the band had any idea of Mercury's worsening condition.

Hiding away in his London mansion, Mercury received news that several of his lovers and ex-boyfriends had passed away from AIDS-related illnesses. Yet he lived in denial, refusing to tell anyone about his condition and allegedly took ten HIV tests in 1986, desperately hoping that the results

A laboratory technician tests blood samples for HIV in 1986, the same year Mercury found out he had the devastating illness.

were wrong. "We talked about other people dying but not about us," said Mercury's longtime friend and collaborator, Peter Straker. "He never talked about those things."[4]

Mercury did, however, speak through his songs. In 1987, he released a cover of the Platters' "The Great Pretender," a popular song from the 1950s. The lyrics go: "Oh yes, I'm the great pretender / Pretending I'm doing well / My need is such, I pretend too much / I'm lonely but no one can tell." Mercury wasn't shy about his connection to the song. "Most of the stuff I do is pretending," he said. "It's like acting. I go on stage and pretend to be a macho man."[5]

The Opera Star

Mercury also embarked on an adventurous new project: a collaboration with a Spanish opera superstar named Montserrat Caballé. During one stop of the tour in Barcelona, Mercury had been asked by a Spanish journalist which singers he most admired, and he had responded with Caballé's name. To his surprise, the opera singer had reached out, and the two ended up meeting at the Ritz Hotel in Barcelona in March 1987.

They started a collaborative relationship, and a few months later, Mercury flew to Ibiza for a surprise appearance at a nightclub where he and Caballé performed a duet that Mercury had written, named after the city where they'd met: "Barcelona." At this point, Mercury had a difficult time hiding the open wounds and lumps that were appearing on his face and body. "There was an incredible party afterwards, and everyone had a good time, but I think we already knew then that Freddie was sick," said the Spanish promoter of the party. "He was not telling anyone anything, but as soon as he arrived we saw that he had begun to get these strange blemishes on his face."[6]

Freddie Mercury and Montserrat Caballé take a photo together in
Ibiza, Spain, May 1987.

Mercury wouldn't be able to keep his condition secret from his band members for much longer. In 1989, Queen returned to the studio to record *The Miracle* and were facing nonstop questions from the press if rumors circulating about Mercury's health were true. One day, they were sitting in a restaurant when Mercury announced, "Look, you've probably figured out what I'm dealing with. I have this thing, and as far as I know there's no cure and I only have a certain time left." Then, he calmly added, "I want life to carry on exactly as it is, I want to make records, I don't want anyone to know, I don't want to anyone to talk about it from this point forwards and that's that."[7]

Everyone at the table was devastated, but they respected Mercury's wishes. "He never asked for sympathy from anyone else," said May. "He was a very strong person and always liked to be in control of his own destiny."[8] In May 1989, *The Miracle* was released and hit number one in the United Kingdom. "We hope to be performing some more miracles for you soon, in 1990 and beyond," said May in his acceptance speech that year at a British awards show, where they'd won Best Band of the Decade.[9] Sadly, it was wishful thinking.

Mercury's Final Weeks

With his body quickly wasting away, Mercury was in a race to get as much work done while he still could. Facing high fevers, nausea, headaches, and indigestion, he struggled through the recording of Queen's next album, *Innuendo*. He often could only record for a few hours every day, but he'd always give it his all. When he didn't have the strength to stand up, he'd even prop himself against the piano, gulp down some vodka, and say, "I'll sing it till I bleed."[10] After many delays, the album was finally released in 1991. It didn't take much to figure out the message behind its lead track, "The Show Must Go On."

AIDS Medication

Even though there is still no cure for AIDS, nowadays there are dozens of different types of drugs to help someone with the virus stay alive. But in the late 1980s, there was only one: AZT. The prohibitively expensive drug cost about $8,000 a year (more than $17,000 today), and the pharmaceutical company that made it, Burroughs Wellcome, was criticized for exploiting vulnerable and desperate patients. Mercury hoped AZT would keep him alive long enough for an AIDS cure. But the reality was that the drug had been overhyped, and there was evidence that it only worked for a limited period of time; in fact, some people taking AZT became even more sick after the virus mutated to resist the drug.[11]

That fall, Mercury decided to stop taking the medications that were keeping him alive. "It was Freddie's decision to finally end it all," said Mary Austin, Mercury's oldest lover and one of his closest friends. "The overwhelming thing for me was that he was just so incredibly brave. He looked death in the face and said, 'Fine, I'll accept it now—I'll go.'"[12]

In September, Mercury turned forty-five, and he celebrated his birthday at his London home with a dinner party attended by a small circle of his closest friends. A few weeks later, he called Queen's manager, Jim Beach, to his home. After a five-hour meeting, Beach emerged with the news that Mercury

The Mystery of Mercury's Final Resting Place

Mercury chose to be cremated after he died, and he entrusted his oldest friend, Mary Austin, to bury his ashes, instructing her to never tell anyone where they were hidden. "I know exactly where I want you to put me. But no one's to know, because I don't want anyone to dig me up," he told her. "I just want to rest in peace."[13] To this day, no one knows where Mercury's final resting place is, although there has been plenty of speculation. In 1991, a plaque was found in London's Kensal Green Cemetery with Farrokh Bulsara, Mercury's birth name, inscribed on it. Still, there is no proof that Mercury's ashes are located there. The mystery remains—just how he wanted it.

wanted to release an official statement to the press confirming that he had AIDS. The night after the news broke to the public, Mercury looked as though a weight had been lifted from his shoulder. A few days later, he slipped into a coma. On November 24, 1991, at 6:48 p.m., Mercury was pronounced dead at his home.

Mercury's death brought much-needed attention to the AIDS crisis in the wider public, especially after his bandmates organized a tribute concert a few weeks after his passing called

Annie Lennox of the Eurythmics and David Bowie perform "Under Pressure" in honor of Freddie Mercury at the April 20, 1992, concert for AIDS awareness.

The Freddie Mercury Tribute: A Concert for AIDS Awareness. Stars such as Elton John, Axl Rose, and George Michael took the stage at Wembley Stadium to perform Queen's classic hits and celebrate Mercury's life and work.

With Mercury gone, the rest of Queen had to figure out what to do with the heaps of vocal work he'd feverishly recorded in his final weeks. They decided to rework this material into their next and final album. Four years after Mercury's death, *Made in Heaven* was released, closing the door on his spectacular career.

Queen's Legacy

Queen's legacy lived on beyond Mercury's death. Several of their old albums resurfaced on the charts throughout the early 1990s, and in 1997, the band's remaining members recorded a tribute to Mercury and all those whose lives had been cut short too soon with a song called "No One But You (Only the Good Die Young)." While Deacon chose to retire and avoid the public spotlight soon after, May and Taylor continued performing and recording songs together. In 2001, Queen was inducted into the Rock and Roll Hall of Fame, sealing their status as one of the greatest rock bands of all time.

Post-Mercury Projects

In 2002, a musical called *We Will Rock You,* which has a fictional plot but is based on Queen's songs, debuted at the Dominion Theatre in London. It received negative reviews but remained so popular that it stayed in production for twelve years, becoming the tenth longest running musical in the history of London's West End, an area renowned for its professional theater shows.

In 2010, May and Taylor announced that they were leaving their longtime record label, EMI. Instead, they signed to Island Records, an arm of Universal Music Group, and rereleased their first five albums to celebrate their fortieth anniversary. "We are very excited, after all this time, to be embarking on a new phase of our career— with a new record company, with new ideas, and new dreams," said May.[1]

Roger Taylor (*left*), Brian May, and Freddie Mercury's mother, Jer Bulsara, attend the Rock and Roll Hall of Fame induction dinner in March 2001, ten years after Mercury's death.

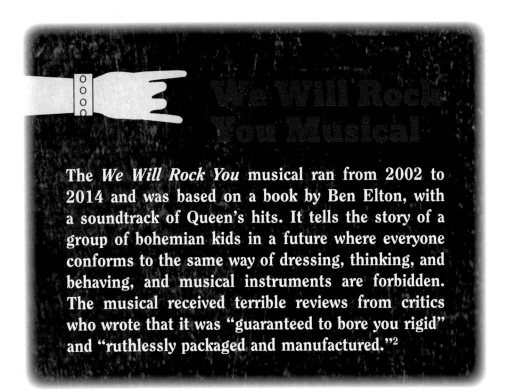

We Will Rock You Musical

The *We Will Rock You* musical ran from 2002 to 2014 and was based on a book by Ben Elton, with a soundtrack of Queen's hits. It tells the story of a group of bohemian kids in a future where everyone conforms to the same way of dressing, thinking, and behaving, and musical instruments are forbidden. The musical received terrible reviews from critics who wrote that it was "guaranteed to bore you rigid" and "ruthlessly packaged and manufactured."[2]

Queen performed at the closing ceremony of the 2012 Summer Olympics in London, opening with a remastered video clip of Mercury onstage calling out to the audience at their 1986 concert at Wembley Stadium. They were later joined by singer Jessie J for a performance of "We Will Rock You."

May and Taylor also continued to collaborate and play shows together, joined by guest singers such as Elton John, Robbie Williams, and even the opera singer Luciano Pavarotti. In 2004, May and Taylor began touring with Paul Rodgers, a close friend who was also the former lead singer of the bands Free and Bad Company. It was the first time Queen had toured

 **"Paul is just such a great singer. He's not trying to be Freddie."**

Actor Rami Malek attends the British Independent Film Awards in 2017. He portrays Freddie Mercury in *Bohemian Rhapsody*, a movie about Queen's rise to fame.

Queen

the world without Mercury. "We never thought we would tour again, but Paul came along by chance and we seemed to have a chemistry," Taylor said. "Paul is just such a great singer. He's not trying to be Freddie."[3]

After years of being riddled with delays and behind-the-scenes issues, the band's biopic, titled *Bohemian Rhapsody*, was finally released November 2, 2018. The film follows Queen from before they started up until their 1985 Live Aid performance. It is directed by Dexter Fletcher and stars Rami Malek as Freddie Mercury, Gwilym Lee as Brian May, Ben Hardy as Roger Taylor, and Joseph Mazzello as John Deacon.[4]

The Adam Lambert Years

Rodgers stopped performing with Queen in 2009, but that same year, they discovered Adam Lambert, a young, flamboyant singer who had auditioned for *American Idol* by performing a cover of "Bohemian Rhapsody." Taylor and May had seen thousands of singers in their lifetimes auditioning for the role of Mercury as part of their *We Will Rock You* musical. But Lambert stood out for his musical range and ability to reinterpret the songs that were so foundational to Queen. "I always think that Freddie, with a wicked smile, would say something like 'I hate you, Madam Lambert,'" said May. "Because even Freddie would have been gobsmacked."[5]

The admiration was mutual with Lambert. "What I always loved about Queen was that I could see what Freddie and the band were exploring, and I could identify with that," he said. "I started falling in love with rock & roll, I dressed up like a club kid and went out at night, I'm gay—all of that stuff put together. When I look at the history of rock & roll, Queen is the band that resonated the most with me: 'That's me, that's my life.'"[6] Years later, the band teamed up with Lambert as their vocalist, and they have been touring together ever since.

Brian May and Adam Lambert play in Inglewood, California, July 2014. Lambert identified with Queen growing up and was thrilled to join his idols on tour.

In 2017, Queen and Adam Lambert debuted a state-of-the-art digital stage production that modernized their show to create a new, immersive rock concert experience. "People will be shocked. It doesn't look traditional at all," said May. "Nevertheless, we'll be able to use it to recreate some moments from the past in some ways, which is going to be fascinating."[7] Their collaboration continues with concerts scheduled through the rest of 2018.

There is no doubt in anyone's mind that no one can or will ever replace Mercury's role in Queen and that the band drew its strength from the four different personalities of each member coming together to create something larger than what they could do individually. With their hybrid of hard rock, pop, heavy metal, cabaret show tunes, and even a dose of opera, Queen was unlike any band that came before them, or after. They paved the way for countless other acts with their elaborate live shows, complex studio productions, and devil-may-care image of playful decadence.

Most of all, Queen, especially Mercury, was a shining example of how far you can go when you give it your all until the very end. Perhaps Mercury summed it up best when he sang these lines during his final weeks on earth, lyrics that ended up in one of their last songs, "Made in Heaven": "I'm playing my role in history, looking to find my goal / Taking in all this misery, but giving it all my soul..."

Timeline

1946 Freddie Mercury is born Farrokh Bulsara on September 5 in Stone Town, Zanzibar (now part of Tanzania).

1947 Brian May is born on July 19 in Middlesex, England.

1949 Roger Taylor is born July 26 in Norfolk, England.

1951 John Deacon is born on August 19 in Leicester, England.

1971 Queen plays their first show on July 2 at a Surrey college outside London.

1973 Queen signs their first contract with Trident/EMI and releases their self-titled debut album.

1974 *Queen II* and *Sheer Heart Attack* are released.

1975 *A Night at the Opera* is released.

1976 *A Day at the Races* is released.

1977 *News of the World* is released.

1978 *Jazz* is released

1980 *The Game* and *Flash Gordon* are released.

1981 *Greatest Hits* is released.

1982 *Hot Space* is released.

1984 *The Works* is released.

1985 Queen plays the Live Aid concert on July 13.

1986 *A Kind of Magic* is released.

1989 *The Miracle* is released.

1991 Freddie Mercury dies at age forty-five from AIDS-related illness on November 24 in London, England.

1992 The Freddie Mercury Tribute Concert is held at London's Wembley Stadium on April 20.

1995 *Made in Heaven* is released.

1997 John Deacon retires from the music industry.

2001 Queen is inducted into the Rock and Roll Hall of Fame.

2003 Queen is inducted into the Songwriters Hall of Fame.

2005 Queen teams up with Paul Rodgers for concerts and tours.

2008 Queen splits with Paul Rodgers.

2009 *Absolute Greatest* is released.

2010 Queen signs with Universal Music.

2011 Queen celebrates their fortieth anniversary by rereleasing their catalog of albums.

2012 Queen performs at the closing ceremony of the 2012 Summer Olympics in London; Queen starts performing with Adam Lambert.

2017 Queen + Adam Lambert embark on a 25-city North American tour.

2018 Queen biopic *Bohemian Rhapsody* is released.

Discography

1973 *Queen*
1974 *Queen II*
         Sheer Heart Attack
1975 *A Night at the Opera*
1976 *A Day at the Races*
1977 *News of the World*
         On Air
1978 *Jazz*
1979 *Live Killers*
1980 *The Game*
         Flash Gordon
1981 *Greatest Hits*
1982 *Hot Space*
1984 *The Works*
1986 *A Kind of Magic*
         Live Magic
1989 *The Miracle*
         At the Beeb
1991 *Innuendo*
         Greatest Hits II
1992 *Live at Wembley '86*
         Classic Queen
1995 *Made in Heaven*
1999 *Greatest Hits III*
2009 *Absolute Greatest*
2013 *Icon*
2014 *Queen Forever*

Chapter Notes

Introduction

1. Fraser Mcalpine, "10 Things You May Not Know About Queen's 'Bohemian Rhapsody,'" BBC America, October 10, 2015, http://www.bbcamerica.com/anglophenia/2015/10/10-things-you-may-not-know-about-queens-bohemian-rhapsody.
2. Jonathan McAloon, "10 Songs Nobody Understands," *Telegraph,* April 7, 2015, http://www.telegraph.co.uk/culture/music/11519641/10-songs-nobody-understands.html.

1
Before They Were Queen

1. Alan Light, "The Life and Times of Metallica and Queen," *New York Times,* June 3, 2011, http://www.nytimes.com/2011/06/05/books/review/the-life-and-times-of-metallica-and-queen.html.
2. Ruth Huntman, "Brian May: Me, My Dad and 'the Old Lady,'" *Guardian,* October 18, 2014, https://www.theguardian.com/lifeandstyle/2014/oct/18/brian-may-queen-guitar-red-special-dad?CMP=ema_630.
3. Ibid.
4. "1984," Queenpedia.com, http://www.queenpedia.com/index.php?title=1984 (accessed March 29, 2018).
5. "Queen in the Sixties," *Record Collector Magazine* (November 1995) found on BrianMay.com, 2017, https://www.brianmay.com/queen/queenbeforequeen/rcnov95/rcnov95.html.
6. "Roger Taylor," *Circus Magazine* (1975) found on FMQ—Freddie Mercury and Queen, 2013, http://www.mercury-and-queen.com/rogertaylor.htm.
7. Jeffrey Hudson, "The Invisible Man," *Bassist and Bass Techniques* (April 1996) found on Deaky.Net, accessed March 29, 2018, http://www.deaky.net/rain/invisibleman-e.html.

2

Early Days

1. Mikal Gilmore, "Queen's Tragic Rhapsody," *Rolling Stone,* July 7, 2014, https://www.rollingstone.com/music/news/queens-tragic-rhapsody-20140707.
2. David Kamp, "The British Invasion," *Vanity Fair,* November 2002, https://www.vanityfair.com/culture/2002/11/british-invasion-oral-history.
3. Gilmore.
4. Jacky Gunn and Jim Jenkins, "As It Began," *Record Collector Magazine* (March 1996) found on Freddie.Ru, http://www.freddie.ru/e/bio/ (accessed March 29, 2018).
5. Ibid.
6. Gilmore.
7. Ibid.
8. Jeffrey Hudson, "The Invisible Man," *Bassist and Bass Techniques* (April 1996) found on Deaky.Net, http://www.deaky.net/rain/invisibleman-e.html (accessed March 29, 2018).
9. Warren Manger, "The Secret Life of Freddie Mercury—Sausage Rolls, Stamp Collecting, Japanese Art, Stray Cats and Shyness," *Daily Mirror,* November 23, 2016, https://www.mirror.co.uk/3am/celebrity-news/secret-life-freddie-mercury-sausage-9321292.

3

The Beginning

1. Norman J. Sheffield, "'Freddie Mercury Felt Like a God. Then He Started Behaving Like One,' by the Man Who Signed Queen," *Daily Mail,* July 20, 2013, http://www.dailymail.co.uk/home/event/article-2368614/Queen-Freddie-Mercury-felt-like-god-Then-started-behaving-like-man-signed-band.html.
2. Ibid.
3. Ibid.
4. "Queen," *Winnipeg Free Press* (January 5, 1974) found on QueenArchives.com, http://www.queenarchives.com/index.

php?title=Queen_-_01-05-1974_-_Queen_-_Winnipeg_Free_Press (accessed March 29, 2018).

5. "New York 5-11-74," Queenlive.ca, updated February 26, 2018, http://queenlive.ca/queen/74-05-11.htm.

6. Ibid.

7. "The 3 Phases of Brian May," *Circus Magazine* (July 6, 1976) found on Queenmusichall.cz, 2018, https://www.queenmusichall.cz/en/interviews/brian-may-circus-magazine-76.html.

4
Killer Queen

1. Caroline Coon, "'I Can Dream Up All Kinds of Things'—A Classic Freddie Mercury Interview from the Vaults," *Guardian,* November 22, 2011, https://www.theguardian.com/music/2011/nov/22/freddie-mercury-interview-rocks-backpages.

2. "11-02-1974 – NME," QueenArchives.com, 2014, http://queenarchives.com/qa/11-02-1974-nme/.

3. Mark Sutherland, "Party On: Queen's Brian May Remembers 'Bohemian Rhapsody' on 40th Anniversary," *Rolling Stone,* October 30, 2015, https://www.rollingstone.com/music/news/party-on-queens-brian-may-remembers-bohemian-rhapsody-on-40th-anniversary-20151030.

4. Jeff Giles, "The Story of Queen's Iconic 'Bohemian Rhapsody' Video," Ultimate Classic Rock, http://ultimateclassicrock.com/queen-bohemian-rhapsody-video/ (accessed March 29, 2018).

5. Matt Richards and Mark Langthorne, *Somebody to Love: The Life, Death and Legacy of Freddie Mercury* (San Francisco, CA: Weldon Owen, 2016), p. 102.

6. Ibid.

7. David Peisner, "The Oral History of the 'Wayne's World' 'Bohemian Rhapsody' Scene," *Rolling Stone,* November 30, 2015, https://www.rollingstone.com/music/news/the-oral-history-of-the-wayne-s-world-bohemian-rhapsody-scene-20151130.

8. Norman J. Sheffield, "'Freddie Mercury Felt Like a God. Then He Started Behaving Like One,' by the Man Who Signed Queen," *Daily Mail,* July 20, 2013, http://www.dailymail.co.uk/home/event/article-2368614/Queen-Freddie-Mercury-felt-like-god-Then-started-behaving-like-man-signed-band.html.
9. Sutherland.

5
Race to the Top

1. "05-02-1981 - Melody Maker," QueenArchives.com, http://www.queenarchives.com/index.php?title=Freddie_Mercury_-_05-02-1981_-_Melody_Maker (accessed March 29, 2018).
2. Matt Richards and Mark Langthorne, *Somebody to Love: The Life, Death and Legacy of Freddie Mercury* (San Francisco, CA: Weldon Owen, 2016), p. 138.
3. Richards and Langthorne, p. 140.
4. Mick Wall, "Stone Cold Crazy: Brian May Interview: Part 3," *Q Classic* (March 2005) found on BrianMay.com, 2017, https://brianmay.com/queen/tour05/interviews/bm_classicq_mar05pt3.html

6
Disco Downfall

1. David Chiu, "How Queen Embraced Disco, Conquered America, Then Bit the Dust," Medium.com, June 24, 2015, https://medium.com/cuepoint/the-game-how-queen-conquered-and-lost-america-a3c48103ac62.
2. Ibid.
3. Ibid.
4. Lesley-Ann Jones, *Mercury: An Intimate Biography of Freddie Mercury* (New York, NY: Touchstone, 2012), p. 174.
5. Mark Blake, *Is This the Real Life? The Untold Story of Queen* (Cambridge, MA: Da Capo Press, 2011), preview, https://books.google.com.

6. Stan, "MUSIC: David Bowie and Members Of Queen Describe Writing Their Hit Song, 'Under Pressure,'" AlterPolitics, December 16, 2012, http://www.alterpolitics.com/arts-entertainment/music-david-bowie-and-members-of-queen-describe-writing-their-hit-song-under-pressure/.

7. Jones, p. 237.

8. Matt Richards and Mark Langthorne, *Somebody to Love: The Life, Death and Legacy of Freddie Mercury* (San Francisco, CA: Weldon Owen, 2016), p. 248.

9. Chiu.

7

"The Greatest Day of Our Lives"

1. Anita Gates, "Television Review; The Epidemic as Avalanche: A Two-Part Series Documents 25 Years of AIDS," *New York Times,* May 30, 2006, http://query.nytimes.com/gst/fullpage.html?res=9B02EEDD1F3EF933A05756C0A9609C8B63.

2. Matt Richards and Mark Langthorne, *Somebody to Love: The Life, Death and Legacy of Freddie Mercury* (San Francisco, CA: Weldon Owen, 2016), p. 102.

3. "Mr. Bad Guy (1985)," Freddiemercury.com, 2018, http://www.freddiemercury.com/en/archive.

4. "LIVE AID 1985: How It All Happened," BBC, http://www.bbc.co.uk/music/thelive8event/liveaid/history.shtml (accessed March 29, 2018).

5. Andy Kershaw, *No Off Switch* (London, UK: Virgin Books, 2012), p. 193.

6. OfficalQueenRomania, "Queen-Interview Before Live Aid 1985," YouTube, May 27, 2014, https://www.youtube.com/watch?v=ltOxVumTcEM.

7. Jon Hotten, "At Her Majesty's Request—Real Life—Or Just Fantasy? Part 2," BrianMay.com, 2017, https://brianmay.com/freddie/cr1201/cr1201b.html.

8. Peter Stanford, "Queen: Their Finest Moment at Live Aid," *Telegraph,* September 24, 2011, http://www.telegraph.co.uk/culture/music/rockandpopmusic/8785536/Queen-their-finest-moment-at-Live-Aid.html.

9. Ibid.

10. Nick Deriso, "How Queen Stole the Show at Live Aid," Ultimate Classic Rock, July 13, 2015, http://ultimateclassicrock.com/queen-live-aid/.

8

Made in Heaven

1. Mark Blake, *Freddie Mercury: A Kind of Magic* (Milwaukee,WI: Backbeat Books, 2016), preview, https://books.google.com.

2. Matt Richards and Mark Langthorne, *Somebody to Love: The Life, Death and Legacy of Freddie Mercury* (San Francisco, CA: Weldon Owen, 2016), p. 281.

3. Lesley-Ann Jones, *Mercury: An Intimate Biography of Freddie Mercury* (New York, NY: Touchstone, 2012), p. 174.

4. Ibid., p. 329.

5. David Wigg, "'For Me, It's the Bigger the Better...in Everything': BBC Documentary Goes Behind the Scenes with the Late, Great Freddie Mercury," *Daily Mail,* October 12, 2012, http://www.dailymail.co.uk/tvshowbiz/article-2216408/BBC-documentary-goes-scenes-late-great-Freddie-Mercury.html#ixzz59OdMnLbD.

6. Laura Jackson, *Freddie Mercury: The Biography* (London, UK: Hachette Digital, 2011), preview, https://books.google.com.

7. Richards and Langthorne, p. 329.

8. *Days of Our Lives*, BBC TV (Globe Productions, 2011).

9. Richards and Langthorne, p. 332.

10. Mikal Gilmore, "Queen's Tragic Rhapsody," *Rolling Stone,* July 7, 2014, https://www.rollingstone.com/music/news/queens-tragic-rhapsody-20140707.

11. Alice Park, "The Story Behind the First AIDS Drug," *Time,* March 19, 2017, http://time.com/4705809/first-aids-drug-azt/.

12. David Wigg, "The Ex-Lover of Freddie Mercury Shares Her Memories of the Late Queen Singer Inside His Home," *OK Magazine,* March 17, 2000, http://www.freddie.ru/e/archives/ok/.

13. Jordan Runtagh, "Freddie Mercury: 10 Things You Didn't Know Queen Singer Did," *Rolling Stone,* November 23, 2016, https://www.rollingstone.com/music/lists/freddie-mercury-10-things-you-didnt-know-queen-singer-did-w451918.

9

Queen's Legacy

1. Bryan Wawzenek, "Queen Switch Record Labels, " Gibson.com, November 9, 2010, http://www.gibson.com/news-lifestyle/news/en-us/queen-1109.aspx.

2. "Raspberries for Queen's Rhapsody," BBC, May 15, 2002, http://news.bbc.co.uk/2/hi/entertainment/1988767.stm.

3. Owen Gibson, "Queen Most Loved Band," *Guardian,* July 5, 2005, https://www.theguardian.com/uk/2005/jul/05/arts.artsnews1.

4. Nick Reilly, "The Release of Queen Biopic 'Bohemian Rhapsody' Has Been Moved Forward," NME, March 27, 2018, http://www.nme.com/news/film/the-release-of-queen-biopic-bohemian-rhapsody-has-been-moved-forward-2274332.

5. Brian May, "Brian May: How Adam Lambert Joined the Queen Family," ClassicRock, November 28, 2017, http://teamrock.com/feature/2017-11-28/brian-may-how-adam-lambert-joined-the-queen-family.

6. Steve Appleford, "How Queen + Adam Lambert Are Keeping Freddie Mercury's Legacy Alive," *Rolling Stone,* February 1, 2017, https://www.rollingstone.com/music/features/queen-adam-lambert-on-honoring-freddie-mercurys-legacy-w464081.

7. Ibid.

Glossary

acclaim Enthusiastic praise.

ballad A story-driven song, usually with romantic themes.

Billboard A leading music magazine that runs the industry's standard music charts.

biopic A biographical movie.

bohemian A free-spirited artist with a nonconformist lifestyle.

decadence Excessive pleasure and luxury.

disco A musical genre that began in the 1970s and features electronic instruments.

flamboyant Extremely confident and stylish.

glam rock A style of rock music known for elaborately dressed performers.

HIV A virus that causes the failure of the human immune system and can lead to AIDS.

impromptu In-the-moment, done without any planning or rehearsal.

legacy A situation that exists because of something that happened in the past.

pander To purposefully satisfy someone's need for something.

psychedelic rock A style of rock music known for its use of feedback, electronics, and high volumes.

renowned Famous, well-known.

rockabilly An early style of rock music from the 1950s that incorporates country elements and is closely associated with Elvis Presley.

Rolling Stone A leading music magazine.

synthesizer An electronic musical instrument first used in pop music in the 1960s.

 # Further Reading

Books

Blake, Mark. *Freddie Mercury: A Kind of Magic*. New York, NY: Omnibus Press, 2016.

Hince, Peter. *Queen Unseen: My Life with the Greatest Rock Band of the 20th Century*. London, UK: John Blake, 2016.

May, Brian, and Simon Bradley. *Brian May's Red Special: The Story of the Home-Made Guitar That Rocked Queen and the World*. London, UK: Carlton Books, 2018.

Philo, Simon, and Scott Calhoun. *Glam Rock: Music in Sound and Vision*. Lanham, Md.: Rowman & Littlefield, 2018.

Reynolds, Simon. *Shock and Awe: Glam Rock and Its Legacy, from the Seventies to the Twenty-First Century*. London, England: Faber and Faber, 2017.

Richards, Matt, and Mark Langthorne. *Somebody to Love: The Life, Death, and Legacy of Freddie Mercury*. London, UK: WeldonOwen, 2016.

Websites

Brian May Official Website
www.brianmay.com
Explore the personal recollections of a key member of Queen.

Freddie Mercury Official Website
www.freddiemercury.com/
Dive deeper into Freddie Mercury's artistic genius by viewing photos and descriptions of his complete works.

Queenpedia
www.queenpedia.com
Read the history and descriptions of each album in Queen's discography.

Films

Queen: *Days of Our Lives* (2011), directed by Matt O'Casey.

Queen: *Rock the World* (2017), directed by Christopher Bird.

Index